creative FINGerFun

Compiled by
Margaret M. Self

G/L
REGAL
BOOKS
™

A Division of G/L Publications
Glendale, California, U.S.A.

Acknowledgment

The finger plays and poems included in this book originated from many different sources. Some have been passed on orally from teacher to teacher. Some have come from children, and some have been composed especially for this book.

Grateful acknowledgment is due Elizabeth Winter for her assistance in the preparation of this book. Poems with the following individual credit are copyrighted 1967, 1971, 1972, 1974 by G/L Publications and may be used only with permission.

Poems by ac	Anne Christenberry
Poems by llc	Lois L. Curley
Poems by jbk	Judith B. Kaiser
Poems by rrm	Rosemary R. Myers
Poems by vps	Valerie P. Seger
Poems by mms	Margaret M. Self
Poems by gs	Gladys Seashore
Poems by mgs	Mildred G. Sholund

Published by
Regal Books Division, G/L Publications
Glendale, California 91209, U.S.A.

Library of Congress Catalog Card No. 73-88992
ISBN 0-8307-0268-7

Contents

OLD TESTAMENT
God Made Our World   **1**
Our World   **2**
Birds   **3**
Because God Loves Me   **4**
God Made Everybody   **5**
God Made Adam   **6**
A Happy Family   **7**
The Big Boat   **8**
When Noah Built the Ark   **9**
I Will Be with You   **10**
Baby Moses   **12**
Thirsty People   **14**
Samuel Helps at Home   **15**
Samuel Helps at Church   **16**
Samuel Listens   **17**
Samuel Helps Choose   **18**
David's Sheep   **19**
Clippety Clop!   **20**
David with His Slingshot   **21**
David and Jonathan   **22**
David   **23**
Sharing Food   **24**
Helping Elisha   **25**
Elisha   **26**
Elisha's Room   **27**
Elisha Helps   **28**
The Church   **29**

We're Helpers **30**
Finding the Bible-Scroll **31**
King Josiah **32**
When Ezra Read the Bible **33**
Everyone Helps **34**
Daniel **35**

NEW TESTAMENT

Mary's Secret **39**
The First Christmas **40**
Baby Jesus **41**
Shepherds on a Quiet Hillside **42**
The Wise Men **43**
Up Hill and Down **44**
Jesus Was a Helper **46**
Jesus Goes to Church **47**
Nighttime Visit **48**
Beside the Well **49**
The Little Boy **50**
Peter's Boat **51**
Peter **52**
Four Fishermen **53**
Four Friends **54**
The Lame Man **55**
In the Church **56**
The Storm **57**
I Must See Jesus **58**
Two Blind Men **59**
Many People **60**
Here Is the Boat **61**
A Happy Mother **62**
Here Is Jesus **63**
So Many People **64**

The Happy Man 65
Jesus Taught His Friends 66
This Is the Lady 67
The Good Shepherd 68
Ten Men 69
Zacchaeus 70
The Children 71
The Happy Parade 72
A Story Jesus Told 73
I Will Come Again 74
The First Easter 75
Peter Helps 76
Helping Others 77
Kind Friends 78
Dorcas 79
Learning of Jesus 80
Paul Told Others 81
Timothy Helps 82
Lydia Shows Love 83
Paul Helps 84

THE BIBLE

Open God's Word 87
Really-So Stories 88
We Read the Bible 88
I See the Bible 89
It's True! 90
The Bible 91
Here Is Our Bible 92

How to Use
Bible Story Finger Fun

"Let's do it again!" suggests Brian as his teacher concludes a Bible story finger fun. Why does Brian find this activity so pleasant that he wants to repeat it?

Bible story finger fun offers Brian and his friends opportunities for—

• Physical activity. A child's growing muscles become tense from sitting still for long periods. He needs a frequent change of pace from quiet learning to active participation.

• Rhythmic experience, so natural for a child. He responds almost intuitively to the measured beats of the words.

• Dramatic play. What better way for a child to know how Bible friends might have felt than to play out the situation! Dramatizing Bible story action also sparks a child's interest in the Bible story itself. The words help a child remember and relate a Bible truth to his own experience.

Like other effective methods to help children learn, Bible story finger fun requires your thoughtful preparation and use. When you plan to use a new Bible story finger fun, you will want to—

1. Study each finger fun until the words and hand movements become thoroughly familiar.

2. Use the same finger fun frequently. How children love repetition! Encourage them to join you, first in the actions, then in the words. (Do not expect very young children to repeat words and actions at the same time. They will simply enjoy hearing and seeing you present the Bible story finger fun.)

3. Remember that little fingers are learning coordination. Each time you use the new finger fun, the children will follow with greater ease and participation.

4. Be enthusiastic! Your interest in the Bible story finger fun is essential. Speak slowly and distinctly, yet rhythmically. Express feelings of the story in your voice and actions. For example, look angry or frightened. Smile a big smile to show happiness.

Old Testament

God Made Our World

GENESIS 1

God made our world, our big, big world,

He made the mountains high.

He made the trees, the tall, tall trees,

He made the birds that fly.

God made the sun, the bright, round sun,

That shines and keeps us warm.

God made our world, our big, big world,

Yes, God has made it all!

—ac

Our World

Do you know our world began

A long, long time ago?

God made our world from nothing;

He spoke and it was so.

Daytime, nighttime, sun and sky,

The moon and stars that glow.

God made our world so beautiful—

Flow'rs growing in the sun,

All animals and birds and fish—

God made them, every one.

—jbk

2

Birds

GENESIS 1:4,5,20

Birds all rest, in their nests,

Flow'rs sleep on the hill.

Hush now, bees! Quiet, trees!

All the world is still.

Moon up high, sailing by,

Spreads its silv'ry light.

Sleepy-head, time for bed,

I'm glad God made night.

—*jbk*

Because God Loves Me

GENESIS 1:21

All the big fish like to be

Underneath the wavy sea.

God made swimming fish, I know

Just because He loves me so.

Big white horses gallop fast

Through the fields of tall, green grass.

God made all of them, I know

Just because He loves me so.

—jbk

God Made Everybody

GENESIS 2:7

Long ago there were no people.

Then God made Adam.

Then God made Eve.

Then God made lots of people.

See the people hurry!

God Made Adam

GENESIS 2:7,18,21–23

God made Adam, God made Eve.

To love God and to love each other.

God said,

"Take care of all the things you see,

And live together happily."

Adam and Eve said to God,

"What you tell us we will do,

For you love us, and we love you."

—jbk

A Happy Family

GENESIS 4:1,2

God made Eve and Adam.

At first there were just two,

Then God sent Cain and Abel,

To four the family grew.

"Such fine boys" said Adam.

He hugged them lovingly

"How glad I am that God planned

Our happy family!"

—jbk

7

The Big Boat

GENESIS 6:19,20

Before Noah's
   big, big, boat
Started on
   that long, long float,

Animals went
   marching in!
Some were fat,
   and some were thin!

Some were short,
   and some were tall,
Some could hop,
   and some could crawl!

Some birds flew,
   some walked inside,
To build their nests
   and to hide.

—vps

When Noah Built the Ark

GENESIS 6:11–14,18,19; 7:17

The Lord told Noah, "Build an ark.

Go build it tall and wide."

So Noah and his boys worked hard

To build the rooms inside.

The animals came two by two;

They marched 'til after dark.

Then Noah's fam'ly went inside

The safety of the ark.

Then God came down and shut the door.

That's what the Bible says.

And Noah's fam'ly in the ark

Was safe for forty days.

—rrm

I Will Be with You

GENESIS 28:11–15

Long, long ago

In a land far away,

Jacob slept soundly

Until it was day.

Up overhead

In the heavens so high

Twinkled the stars

In the quiet night sky.

Jacob was dreaming:

There came a great light,

Angels, a ladder—

All shining and bright.

God, our dear Father,

Was standing there, too,

Promising Jacob,

"I'll watch over you."

God makes this promise

For us here today:

"I will be with you,"*

He tells us, "always."

—llc

*Matthew 28:20

Baby Moses

EXODUS 1:22; 2:1–10

God's people lived in Egypt.

There were so many,

The king was afraid they would

Take over his land.

"Throw their babies in the river!"

The king told his soldiers.

Mother Jochebed tried to hide Baby Moses.

But he wiggled, and giggled,

And cried.

She asked God what to do.

God gave her an idea.

She made a basket-bed.

She covered it with tar

So it would float.

She put Moses inside,

And closed the lid.

She put the basket-boat in the river.

Big sister hid in the grass to watch.

The king's daughter came along.

She heard Baby Moses crying.

She opened the basket.

"What a sweet baby," she said.

"I will keep him for my own."

Big sister ran home to tell mother.

"Thank you, God, for keeping Moses safe,"

Said his mother.

Thirsty People

EXODUS 15:27

"The sun is hot!" the people groaned,

"And we are thirsty, too."

Moses listened. Then he said,

"God's taking care of you."

The thirsty people traveled on,

Then someone shouted, "See

Those tall trees and springs nearby!"

They hurried on quickly.

And sure enough there were some trees,

And springs of water, too.

The people drank and Moses said,

"Yes, God took care of you."

—mms

14

Samuel Helps at Home

1 SAMUEL 1:24

On go-to-church day
  with so much to do,
Samuel could help.
  He liked helping, too.
He jumped out of bed;
  and put on his clothes.
He fastened his shoes
  Up over his toes.
He first washed his hands,
  and then his face.
He rolled up his mat
  and put it in place.
He brought in the water;
  ate all his food,
Helped feed the donkey.
  What fun being good!
He held donkey's ropes;
  scratched by each ear.
Mother said, "Good!
  You're a helper, my dear."
Inside the tent-church
  Samuel prayed,
"I'm glad I came
  to the tent-church today."

—jbk

15

Samuel Helps at Church

1 SAMUEL 2:18,26

On help-in-church days with so much to do,

Samuel could help. He liked helping, too.

He put on his clothes early each day.

Rolled up his mat in just the right way.

He polished the candlesticks shiny and bright,

Put oil in the lamps; turned up the lights.

He dusted the tables, swept up the floors.

When all was ready, he opened the doors.

And in the evenings he learned Bible words.

He helped in the tent-church. He pleased the Lord.

—jbk

Samuel Listens

1 SAMUEL 3:1–10

"Samuel! Samuel!" a voice said.

Samuel ran to Eli's bed.

"I did not call you," Eli said

"Please go back into your bed."

Each time the voice called, Samuel came

But Eli said, "I didn't call your name.

"God is calling you, it's clear.

When He calls, say, 'I am here.' "

"Samuel! Samuel!" The voice was near.

Samuel answered, "I am here."

God told Samuel to obey.

Samuel helped in every way.

—jbk

17

Samuel Helps Choose

1 SAMUEL 16:6–13

God told Samuel, "Choose a man

To rule my people and their land."

Samuel looked at Jesse's sons

Which fine boy was God's right one?

The oldest? No! The tallest? No!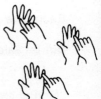

The kindest? No! The shortest? No!

The bravest? No! The strongest? No!

Then came David, fair and tall.

He loved God most of all.

"David's the one!" the Lord God said.

So Samuel poured oil on David's head.

—jbk

18

David's Sheep

1 SAMUEL 16:11,12

Close your eyes and nod your heads,

Soft and woolly sheep.

David's taking care of you,

Sle-ep, sle-ep, sleep.

David knows the things you need,

Soft and woolly sheep.

He will find you *grass to eat

Sle-ep, sle-ep, sleep.

—jbk

*Repeat finger fun using "water to drink" or "places to rest."

Clippety Clop!

1 SAMUEL 17:17–20

Clippety, cloppety, clop! clop! clop!

Donkey's trotting feet.

David is visiting his brothers three,

Taking food to eat.

"Thanks," said his brothers to David,

"Thank you for our food."

"I'm so glad I can help," David said.

"I like to help you."

—jbk

David with His Slingshot

1 SAMUEL 17:33–37,41–49

David with his slingshot

Killed a great big bear,

Then he killed a lion too,

When it came too near.

David with his slingshot

Hit Goliath's head.

Down that wicked giant came—

Falling down—dead!

Just David with his slingshot?

NO! Here's the secret to it.

He prayed that God would guide the stone

Before he ever threw it.

—gs

21

David and Jonathan

1 SAMUEL 18:1-4

David and Jonathan were good friends,

Playing as all good friends do.

Jonathan gave David his (pretty coat*)

Saying, "Take this. I love you."

—jbk

*Repeat finger fun using "pretty belt," or "bow and arrows."

22

David

2 SAMUEL 9:6,7

David was sad—His good friend was dead.

Now David was King, a crown on his head.

"How can I show that I loved Jonathan?

I know!" he said, "I'll be kind to his son."

Mephibosheth bowed. David lifted his hand,

"I want to give you some horses and land.

I'll give you some clothing; I'll give you some food,

I want to share now what I have with you."

—jbk

23

Sharing Food

1 KINGS 17:11-16

Mother went at supper time

To bake a loaf of bread.

"I've only flour and oil enough

For one more loaf," she said.

Then Elijah said to her,

"Oh, please give me some bread,"

"I can bake just one more loaf,

But I will share," she said.

She gave Elijah her last loaf,

Then God helped her this way,

For she had enough flour and oil

To make more bread each day.

—jbk

24

Helping Elisha

2 KINGS 4:8

Walk, walk, walk, Elisha walked,

Up tall hills and down;

Came at last on one hot day

To little dusty town.

"Come in and rest," a lady called,

"And have a bite to eat.

"Oh, please sit down in our cool house

I'll cook a special treat!"

Elisha rested in the house,

He ate good food that day.

''Thank you so much,'' Elisha said,

And he walked on his way.

—jbk

Elisha

2 KINGS 4:9,10

Elisha the preacher

Was walking one day.

A lady said, "Come to my

House, please, and stay.

I'll build you a room

That is only for you."

"God bless you, kind lady,"

Elisha then said.

Elisha's Room

2 KINGS 4:9,10

Here is Elisha
  with tired, aching feet,
He wants to rest
  from the dust and the heat,
And here is a lady
  so good and so kind,
She has a surprise
  for Elisha to find.

Then up the steps
  to the roof top they go,
She opens the door,
  a fine room now to show.
Here is a bed
  for Elisha to rest,
Here is a fine stool
  for her welcome guest.

Here is a table
  on which he can write,
Here is a lamp
  he can use for his light.
Thank you, dear lady,
  for kindness this day,
Thank you for building
  this fine place to stay.

—jbk

27

Elisha Helps

2 KINGS 4:18-20,32-37

Little sick boy

Put his hand on his head.

He felt quite sick,

And then soon he was dead.

Mother ran fast,

Asked Elisha to come.

He hurried up

To his cool rooftop room.

Prayed to the Lord,

And then he touched the boy,

Who came back alive.

What gladness and joy!

—jbk

The Church

The church was dirty and broken.

The king called all the people;

And they came to help fix God's house.

They sawed.

They pounded.

They sewed.

And they fixed God's house again!

We're Helpers

2 CHRONICLES 24:4,12,13

"Our church is dirty and broken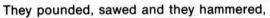

It really looks quite bad,"

The king said to all the people.

His face was oh, so sad.

The people brought many love gifts,

To fix the church like new.

They pounded, sawed and they hammered,

They sewed new curtains, too.

At last the church was all finished,

The painting, too was done.

The happy people all shouted,

"We're helpers, everyone."

—jbk

30

Finding the Bible-Scroll

2 CHRONICLES 34:14

Here is the king,

Here is his crown.

Here is his church,

All broken down.

Here are the helpers,

Who sweep, sew, pound.

An old Bible-scroll

The minister found.

Here's what the king said,

When this news he heard,

"We are so glad

That you found God's words."

—jbk

31

King Josiah

2 CHRONICLES 34:19–21,29–33

When King Josiah read God's words,

He looked very sad.

"Oh, I have not obeyed God's words,

That is very bad."

He said to all the people, "Come,

And listen to God's words."

The people came. They listened. They

Were sad at what they heard.

Then the king and everyone

Promised on that day,

"We'll do what is right and good,

God's words we will obey."

—jbk

32

When Ezra Read the Bible

EZRA 10:1-5

When Ezra read the Bible,

Everyone sat still.

They listened quietly.

Then they said,

"Thank you, dear God,

For the Bible.

We will obey

Your Word."

Everyone Helps

NEHEMIAH 2:17–20

The city's wall was broken down,

The gates were broken, too.

Nehemiah said to everyone,

"Let's build our wall all new."

The fathers cut and laid big stones,

And made gates out of wood.

The children carried water cool,

The mothers cooked good food.

And after they worked very hard,

The new wall was all done,

"We're glad we helped to build our wall,"

They said to everyone.

—jbk

34

Daniel

DANIEL 6

Daniel was so brave and bold

He would not bow to pray

To the king or any man,

But worshiped God each day.

Then wicked men watched Daniel

And threw him in a den.

They thought the lions would eat him,

But God took care of him.

—gs

New Testament

Mary's Secret

LUKE 1:26–31,34,35

Mary was praying,

a bright angel came.

"You'll soon have a baby,

Lord Jesus His name."

"And who is His father?"

"The Lord God above.

He's sending dear Jesus

to show His great love."

Oh, wonderful secret!

The good news was true.

For God sent dear Jesus

to love me and you!

—jbk

39

The First Christmas

LUKE 2:1–7

This is kind Joseph,

And this is sweet Mary;

She rides, and he walks

On their Bethlehem journey.

Here is the inn—

Joseph knocks on the door;

But the innkeeper says,

"No room for more!

Because you are tired,

And 'tis late in the day

You may go to the stable

And rest on clean hay."

'Twas there in the stable

That first Christmas morn,

Jesus, our Saviour,

God's own Son, was born.

—llc

The Baby Jesus

LUKE 2:7

Who loves little baby Jesus?

His mother loved him,

Joseph loved him,

The shepherds loved him,

The wise men loved him,

And I love him.

Do you love him, too?

Shepherds on a Quiet Hillside

LUKE 2:8–17

Shepherds on a quiet hillside

Watched their woolly sheep one night.

Suddenly, a light shone 'round them;

Near them stood an angel bright.

"Do not be afraid," he told them.

"Glad good news to you I bring.

Born this day in Bethlehem,

Baby Jesus, Saviour-King."

Many angels joined in saying,

"Peace on earth, good will to men."

Then the angel left the shepherds

And the sky was dark again.

Shepherds hurried to the city;

Found the babe and manger-bed.

Lovingly they looked at Jesus.

"Surely God loved us," they said.

The Wise Men

MATTHEW 2:9–11

Clop! clop! clop! go the camel's feet,

Clop! clop! clop! on the sand.

Wise men foll'wing a shining star,

To a faraway land.

Where, oh, where is the little one

Who is born to be king?

We are coming to show our love.

These are the gifts that we bring.

Look! look! look! in the sky above,

Look! the star has stopped now.

In the house is God's special one,

We will love Him just now.

—jbk

43

Up Hill and Down

LUKE 2:22–24

Up hill and down

    To Jerusalem town

    Went sweet Mary,

    Kind Joseph and Jesus.

This was the day,

    The first wonderful day,

    That they traveled to their

    Church with Jesus.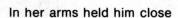

Mary loved him;

    In her arms held him close

    And she thanked God for sending

    Dear Jesus.

Up hill and down

To a faraway town

Went sweet Mary,

Kind Joseph and Jesus.

Mary loved him!

And was thankful that God

Always helped her to care for

Dear Jesus.

Joseph loved him

And was happy that he

Could help Mary take care of

Dear Jesus.

—llc

45

Jesus Was a Helper

LUKE 2:40

Jesus was a helper.

Helped Joseph all He could.

He hammered boards and swept the floors.

And polished chairs of wood.

Jesus was a helper.

Brought water fresh and cold,

Carried sticks for Mother's fire.

He did as He was told.

Jesus was a helper.

Such loving things He'd do.

When we do kind and loving things,

Then we are helpers, too.

—jbk

Jesus Goes to Church

LUKE 2:41,42

Getting ready to go to church,

Jesus helped all He could,

Rolled His blanket and gathered sticks.

Helped Mother pack the food.

Step-step, steppity, step, step, step.

They walked so very far.

At night they camped, built a fire, and ate.

Slept 'neath twinkling stars.

And then they came to the temple-church.

So much they saw and heard.

They sang, they prayed and then best of all

They listened to God's Word.

—jbk

Nighttime Visit

JOHN 3:1–14

Bright stars twinkling in the sky,

Nighttime breezes blowing by,

Nicodemus took a walk,

Came to Jesus for a talk.

Nicodemus said:

"You came to us from God, I know,

To heal the sick, and blind, 'tis so.

Are you the One God said he'd send

To be our Helper, Saviour, Friend?"

Then Jesus said:

"If you believe that I'm God's Son,

Who came to show love for each one,

Then you can be in God's fam'ly,

And God's own child you'll ever be."

—jbk

Beside the Well

JOHN 4:7–15

Step, step, step. The sun was hot.

Jesus said, "It's time to stop."

"I am tired and thirsty, too."

Jesus thought just what to do.

A woman came with jar on head.

"Give me a drink, please," Jesus said.

Jesus talked. The woman heard.

"God loves you," were Jesus' words.

—jbk

The Little Boy

JOHN 4:46–54

"Jesus, come quickly!"

a sad father said.

"My boy is so sick,

he must stay in bed."

How the Lord Jesus

loved this worried man!

"Your boy is now well."

To home Father ran.

Yes, his boy was all well!

Oh, happy day!

Jesus had helped him

this wonderful way.

—jbk

Peter's Boat

LUKE 5:1–3

This is Jesus,

This is the crowd

That followed Him all of the while.

This is Peter,

This is the boat

He shared with a big, happy smile.

—jbk

Peter

LUKE 5:1–7

Peter, the fisherman

Pulled in his net.

Said to his brother,

"No fish did we get."

Then the Lord told him,

"Go try again."

This time the big net

Was filled to the brim.

—gs

Four Fishermen

MATTHEW 4:18–22

Jesus went walking

One day by the sea.

To four fishermen

.

He called, "Come, follow me."

The four fishermen

Brought their boats to the shore,

Jumped out, followed Jesus,

Went fishing no more.

—jbk

Four Friends

MARK 2:1–12

Once there was a sick man,

Who lay upon his bed.

This unhappy sick man

Could not lift up his head.

He had four friends who loved him,

They knew just what to do.

They made a big hole in the roof,

And let the sick man through.

Then Jesus said, ''Pick up your mat.''

The sick man then obeyed.

His legs were strong and he could walk.

He thanked the Lord that day.

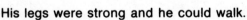

—jbk

The Lame Man

JOHN 5:2-9

Beside the pool a lame man lay.

And he'd lain there every day.

"Oh, how I wish that I could walk!"

The poor lame man would say.

"Get up!" said Jesus to the man.

"Pick up your bed and walk!"

He stood, rolled up his mat and left,

Just too surprised to talk!

When Jesus saw him in the church

Where he had gone to pray,

The man said, "Oh, I thank you, Lord,

For helping me today."

—jbk

In the Church

MATTHEW 12:9–13

In the church there sat a man

With a weak and wrinkled hand.

In came Jesus and He said,

"Hold out your hand. Don't be afraid."

The man reached out; it wasn't long,

Til BOTH his hands were well and strong.

—jbk

The Storm

MARK 4:35-41

Rock, rock, gently rock,

Small boat sails along.

Rest, rest, Jesus rests,

Night wind comes up strong.

Blow, blow, big winds blow,

Toss the waves up high!

Splash! Splash! Waters crash.

"Help! We'll sink! We'll die!"

Wake, wake, Jesus wakes.

"Help you? Yes, I will.

Hush, hush, wild wind, hush!"

All is calm and still.

—jbk

I Must See Jesus

LUKE 8:43–48

"I must see Jesus,"

A sick lady cried.

"No one has helped me,

Though many have tried."

She touches Jesus' coat,

Her hurt place is well.

"Who touched me?" calls Jesus.

"I did, Lord," she tells.

"I helped you because

You believed that I could."

"Oh, thank you, Lord Jesus.

You're kind and you're good."

—jbk

Two Blind Men

MATTHEW 9:27–31

Two blind men
heard people shouting one day,
"Jesus is coming,"
they heard people say.

"Tell us where Jesus is,"
both blind men said.
"Jesus is in that house
right straight ahead."

Both blind men hurried
as fast as could be,
"Jesus, please help us.
Oh, help us to see."

Then Jesus touched their eyes.
Now they could see!
"Thank you, Lord," each said,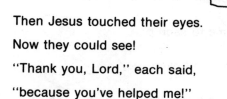
"because you've helped me!"

—mms

Many People

JOHN 6:1–14

Many people came to hear

Jesus talk one day.

Then they were hungry! What to do?

Jesus knew a way.

A little boy gave Him his lunch

Of fish and loaves of bread.

Jesus took the lunch and then,

"Thank you, God," He said.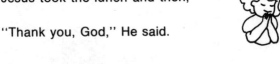

Then Jesus broke the fish and bread

And gave some to each one.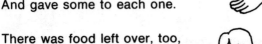

There was food left over, too,

When everyone was done.

—mms

Here Is the Boat

MATTHEW 14:22–27

Here is the boat rocking from side to side.

Here is the wind blowing Ooooooo!

And Jesus' helpers are rowing so hard,

They wish they knew what to do.

Here is Lord Jesus. He's coming to help.

He's walking on top of the sea!

His helpers are so surprised.

Oh, how could such a thing be!

Then Jesus climbs in the little boat, too.

He helps in a wonderful way.

The wind and the water are quiet and still—

His helpers no longer afraid.

—mms

A Happy Mother

MARK 7:24b–30

Many places Jesus went

A mother followed, too.

"Help my sick girl please," she said,

"For you know what to do."

Then Jesus stopped and listened.

He saw that she was sad.

"Go home," He said, "Your girl is well."

Now this mother was glad.

—mms

62

Here Is Jesus

MARK 7:31–37

Here is Jesus, Here's the crowd,

Here are the friends who came.

Here is the man who couldn't hear,

Who couldn't speak his name.

Here is the way Jesus helped:

He touched both tongue and ears.

Here's how the man's big smile spread out;

Now he could speak and hear!

Here are the people, so surprised!

Here's how they ran to tell,

"Jesus can do everything.

He made a deaf man well!"

—jbk

So Many People

MATTHEW 15:32–39

So many people!
To Jesus they came.
Some who were blind
and then some who were lame.
The Lord Jesus made them well;
then to have food,
"Sit down on the grass,"
Jesus said to each one.

He took little fishes,
a few loaves of bread,
And then to the Lord God
a "thank you" He said.
He broke up the bread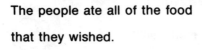
and the few little fish.
The people ate all of the food
that they wished.

—jbk

The Happy Man

JOHN 9:1–12

A blind man sat beside the road.

He could not see the sky.

He could not see the flow'rs or trees,

He could not see birds fly.

Then Jesus put mud on his eyes.

"Go now and wash quickly."

The Blind man did as Jesus said.

He shouted, "I can see!"

"Oh, thank you, Jesus," said the man.

"Thank you for helping me.

My eyes are not blind anymore

I'm so glad I can see!"

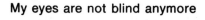

—jbk

Jesus Taught His Friends

LUKE 11:1–4

The sun came up and all was still,

So Jesus woke and climbed the hill.

He liked to talk to God each day.

He liked to bow His head and pray.

His friends said, "Please, teach us to pray,

And tell us now, the words to say."

Jesus taught them what to say.

Jesus taught them how to pray.

—*jbk*

This Is the Lady

LUKE 13:10–13

This is the lady, (her back was so bent)

Walking to her church one day.

"Jesus is here! Oh, yes, Jesus is here!"

She heard the people all say.

Inside the church Jesus read from God's Word.

All listened so carefully.

Then Jesus said to the lady that day,

"Please come and stand here by me."

Then Jesus touched her. And right at that time

She stood up as tall as could be.

"Thank you, dear Jesus, my back is all straight!

I'm so glad you have helped me."

—jbk

The Good Shepherd

One woolly sheep went out skipping along,

Away from the shepherd and sheep.

Then he fell down and was lost in the night,

While others went home and to sleep.

The shepherd went out and looked for his sheep.

He climbed up and down over boulders.

He found that tired sheep and lifted him up,

Then carried him home on his shoulders.

Ten Men

LUKE 17:11–19

Ten poor men sat by the road;

Sick, alone and sad.

Jesus came! He made them well—

Now these men were glad.

Ten glad men went running home,

"Now back to friends we'll go!"

One man stopped. To Jesus said—

"I'm glad you helped me so!"

—jbk

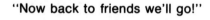

Zacchaeus

LUKE 19:1–10

Zacchaeus heard the people say,

"Jesus is coming here today."

Zacchaeus thought, "What will I do?"

"For I want to see Jesus, too."

He thought of just the way to see.

Zacchaeus climbed up in a tree!

When Jesus saw him in the tree,

He said, "Please come down here to me."

"I want to be your friend today."

And quickly Zacchaeus obeyed.

—mms

The Children

JOHN 12:12–16

Many children went to see Jesus.

Some children walked.

Some children ran.

Some children skipped.

All the children clapped their hands.

They were happy to see Jesus.

—jbk

The Happy Parade

JOHN 12:12–16

Here is the donkey

Clip-clopping along,

Here are the children

They're singing a song.

Here are the branches;

Oh, see how they sway!

Here is Lord Jesus

On this happy day.

—jbk

A Story Jesus Told

MATTHEW 25:14–30

Once Jesus told a story
About three servants who
Were given coins of money
And weren't told what to do.

Two servants used their money well.
They earned more money, too.
They worked quite hard and did their best,
That's what good workers do!

The third servant was lazy,
He did not work a bit!
He buried his money in the ground,
And made no use of it!

Which of these three servants
Would Jesus like to see?
Which of these three servants
Would YOU like to be?

—mms

73

I Will Come Again

JOHN 14:3

God gave me—

Two eyes to see

A tall, tall tree;

And Mother

To take care of me.

A nose to smell

The fragrant flowers;

Two feet that run

And jump for hours.

The best of all

That God has giv'n

Is Jesus, who now

Lives in heav'n.

He promised,

"I will come again."

I'm glad to think I'll see him then.

—mms

The First Easter

JOHN 20:11–18

Mary walked to the garden.

She looked all around.

But her dear friend Jesus—

Could nowhere be found.

Then as Mary was turning

A kind voice she heard.

"Mary!" said the man,

And it was the Lord!

Mary was very happy!

She ran all the way,

To tell, "Jesus is living,"

That first Easter day.

—jbk

Peter Helps

ACTS 3:1–10

John and Peter went to church

As they had done before.

Then they saw a poor lame man,

Beside the big church door.

"Stand up and walk, in Jesus' name!"

Said Peter to the man.

He jumped right up! He stood! He walked!

Into the church he ran.

He said, "Thank you for helping me,

To stand up straight and tall."

Then Peter said, " 'Tis Jesus who

Can do good things for all."

—jbk

Helping Others

ACTS 9:1–6,19–22

As Paul rode on his horse one day,

He saw the light shine brightly,

He heard a voice from heaven say,

"Oh, why don't you love me?"

Yes, it was Jesus' voice Paul heard.

But no one could he see.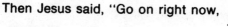

Then Jesus said, "Go on right now,

Help others learn of me."

Paul loved Jesus from that day,

Paul thought just what to do.

Paul helped other people know

That Jesus loved them, too.

—jbk

77

Kind Friends

ACTS 9:23–25

When Paul told of Jesus

Some people were glad.

They smiled and were happy,

But some were quite mad.

They wanted to hurt Paul,

But Paul's friends helped him,

They found a big basket,

And Paul climbed right in.

Friends lowered the basket

Down over the wall.

When it touched ground safely

Out climbed their friend Paul!

—jbk

78

Dorcas

ACTS 9:36

This lady is Dorcas,

Gentle and good.

She helped little children

All that she could.

When a child had no coat,

Or his was all torn,

Dorcas made a new one

To keep him so warm.

—jbk

Learning of Jesus

ACTS 10:23–29

"I want to learn of Jesus,"

Cornelius said one day.

"I wonder just what I should do."

God helped him know a way.

Peter helped Cornelius learn,

And his whole family.

They were glad when Peter said,

"Jesus loves you and me!"

—jbk

Paul Told Others

ACTS 13:47–49; 14

When Paul told others of the Lord

Some were glad to know.

But other people said to Paul,

"We want you to go."

They picked up stones and threw at Paul.

He fell down on the ground.

But God helped Paul get up again,

And go to other towns.

So Paul told people far and near,

"God made each one of you.

He loves you and He is so glad

For you to love Him too."

—mms

Timothy Helps

ACTS 16:1-3

"Will you be my helper?"

Paul asked Timothy.

"Tell others of Jesus,

Will you go with me?"

Young Timothy smiled as

He said, "Yes, I'll go,

To help others know Jesus

Loves each one so."

—jbk

Lydia Shows Love

ACTS 16:14,15

Walking or riding or trotting,

Sailing through waves up and down.

Paul told the people of Jesus

Trav'ling in city and towns.

Lydia heard about Jesus.

"Stay and tell others," she said.

"I want to show love for Jesus.

Please stay at my home!" So they did.

—jbk

Paul Helps

ACTS 27:18–25

Paul and some people

went sailing one day,

On a ship

out in the sea.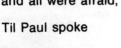

A big wind came blowing

and all were afraid,

Til Paul spoke

so quietly.

"Don't be afraid,"

Paul said to everyone.

"God's taking care

of us now."

Their ship broke apart,

but not one man was lost,

All got to land

safe and sound.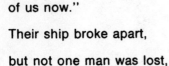

—jbk

The Bible

Open God's Word

This is God's Word, the Bible,

Open its pages wide;

"All things were made by God"*

Is what I read inside.

This is God's Word, the Bible,

Open its pages wide;

"God sent his dear Son, Jesus"

Is what I read inside.

This is God's Word, the Bible,

Open its pages wide;

"God loves children everywhere"

Is what I read inside.

This is God's Word, the Bible,

Open its pages wide;

"Children, obey your parents"

Is what I read inside.

—mgs

*Substitute other Bible verses such as "Go . . . and teach all nations," "Do that which is right and good," "I will sing unto the Lord."

We Read the Bible

When we read the Bible

Everyone sits still.

We listen quietly.

Then we say,

''Thank you, dear God, for the Bible.''

Really-So Stories

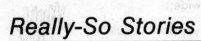

Our Bible-book stories

Are all really so!

They tell us the things

That God wants us to know.

Let's open our ears,

And let's open our eyes,

All ready? Let's look

At a picture surprise!

—jbk

I See the Bible

Here on the table

A Bible I see.

And in its pages

God says he loves ME!

I hold my Bible

And carefully look.

God says he loves YOU!

—Right here in his book.

Open your Bible;

Now open it wide.

Jesus loves children*

These words are inside.

—llc

*Mothers, fathers, fam'lies may be substituted for children.

89

It's True

The Bible says that Jesus died

For me—and you—and you.

The Bible says he is alive!

It's true! It's true! It's true!

The Bible says that Jesus lives;

He sees us while we play;

He cares for us when we're asleep;

He listens when we pray!

The Bible says that Jesus loves

Us all—yes, me—and you.

And someday he will come again!

It's true! It's true! It's true!

—jbk

The Bible

This book is the Bible—

'Tis God's holy Word;

I open its pages

To stories I've heard.

I like to hear stories

Of Jesus, God's Son—

I thank God for giving

His Word for each one.

—*llc*

Here Is Our Bible

Here is our Bible,

Its stories are true!

God gave us these stories

For me and you.

Quiet, so quiet

We all now will be.

Listen!—A story!—

And pictures to see!

Alphabetical Index

A Happy Family, 7
A Happy Mother, 62
A Story Jesus Told, 73

Baby Jesus, The, 41
Baby Moses, 12
Because God Loves Me, 4
Beside the Well, 49
Bible, The 91
Big Boat, The, 8
Birds, 3

Children, The, 71
Church, The, 29
Clippety Clop!, 20

Daniel, 35
David, 23
David and Jonathan, 22
David with His Slingshot, 21
David's Sheep, 19
Dorcas, 79

Elisha, 26
Elisha Helps, 28
Elisha's Room, 27
Everyone Helps, 34

Finding the Bible-Scroll, 31
First Christmas, The, 40
First Easter, The, 75
Four Fishermen, 53
Four Friends, 54

God Made Adam, 6
God Made Everybody, 5
God Made Our World, 1
Good Shepherd, The, 68

Happy Man, The, 65
Happy Parade, The, 72
Helping Elisha, 25
Helping Others, 77
Here Is Jesus, 63
Here Is Our Bible, 92
Here Is the Boat, 61

I Must See Jesus, 58
I See the Bible, 89

I Will Be with You, 10
I Will Come Again, 74
In the Church, 56
It's True!, 90

Jesus Goes to Church, 47
Jesus Taught His Friends, 66
Jesus Was a Helper, 46

Kind Friends, 78
King Josiah, 32

Lame Man, The, 55
Learning of Jesus, 80
Little Boy, The, 50
Lydia Shows Love, 83

Many People, 60
Mary's Secret, 39

Nighttime Visit, 48

Open God's Word, 87
Our World, 2

Paul Helps, 84
Paul Told Others, 81
Peter, 52
Peter's Boat, 51
Peter Helps, 76

Really-So Stories, 88

Samuel Helps at Church, 16
Samuel Helps at Home, 15
Samuel Helps Choose, 18
Samuel Listens, 17
Sharing Food, 24
Shepherds on a Quiet Hillside, 42
So Many People, 64
Storm, The, 57

Ten Men, 69
Thirsty People, 14
This Is the Lady, 67
Timothy Helps, 82
Two Blind Men, 59

Up Hill and Down, 44

We Read the Bible, 88
We're Helpers, 30
When Ezra Read the Bible, 33
When Noah Built the Ark, 9
Wise Men, The, 43

Zacchaeus, 70

Character Index

ADAM AND EVE
God Made Adam, 6
God Made Everybody, 5
Happy Family, A, 7
BLIND MAN AT THE POOL OF SILOAM, THE
Happy Man, The, 65
CANAANITE MOTHER, THE
Happy Mother, A, 62
CHILDREN OF ISRAEL, THE
Thirsty People, 14
CORNELIUS
Learning of Jesus, 80
CRIPPLED MAN, THE
Four Friends, 54
DANIEL
Daniel, 35

97

DAVID
Clippety Clop!, 20
David, 23
David and Jonathan, 22
David with His Slingshot, 21
David's Sheep, 19

DEAF AND MUTE MAN, THE
Here Is Jesus, 63

DORCAS
Dorcas, 79

ELIJAH
Sharing Food, 24

ELISHA
Elisha, 26
Elisha Helps, 28
Elisha's Room, 27
Helping Elisha, 25

EZRA
When Ezra Read the Bible, 33

JACOB
I Will Be with You, 10

JESUS AS A BOY
Jesus Goes to Church, 47
Jesus Was a Helper, 46

JESUS' HELPERS
Four Fishermen, 53

JOASH
Church, The, 29
We're Helpers, 30

JOSIAH
Finding the Bible-Scroll, 31
King Josiah, 32

LAME MAN, THE
  Lame Man, The, 55
LYDIA
  Lydia Shows Love, 83
MAN WITH THE WITHERED HAND, THE
  In the Church, 56
MOSES
  Baby Moses, 12
NEHEMIAH
  Everyone Helps, 34
NICODEMUS
  Nighttime Visit, 48
NOAH
  Big Boat, The, 8
  When Noah Built the Ark, 9
NOBLEMAN'S SON, THE
  Little Boy, The 50
PAUL
  Helping Others, 77
  Kind Friends, 78
  Paul Helps, 84
  Paul Told Others, 81
PETER
  Peter, 52
  Peter's Boat, 51
  Peter Helps, 76
SAMUEL
  Samuel Helps at Church, 16
  Samuel Helps at Home, 15
  Samuel Helps Choose, 18
  Samuel Listens, 17
SICK WOMAN, THE
  I Must See Jesus, 58

TEN LEPERS, THE
  Ten Men, 69
TIMOTHY
  Timothy Helps, 82
TWO BLIND MEN, THE
  Two Blind Men, 59
WOMAN AT THE WELL, THE
  Beside the Well, 49
WOMAN WITH THE BENT BACK
  This Is the Lady, 67
ZACCHAEUS
  Zacchaeus, 70

Topical Index

BIBLE, THE
  Bible, The, 91
  Here Is Our Bible, 92
  I See the Bible, 89
  It's True!, 90
  Open God's Word, 87
  Really-So Stories, 88
  We Read the Bible, 88
CALMING THE SEA
  Storm, The, 57
CHRISTMAS
  Baby Jesus, The, 41
  First Christmas, The, 40
  Mary's Secret, 39
  Shepherds on a Quiet Hillside, 42
  Up Hill and Down, 44
  Wise Men, The, 43

CREATION
  Because God Loves Me, 4
  Birds, 3
  God Made Our World, 1
  Our World, 2
FEEDING THE 4,000
  So Many People, 64
FEEDING THE 5,000
  Many People, 60
LORD'S PRAYER, THE
  Jesus Taught His Friends, 66
PALM SUNDAY
  Children, The, 71
  Happy Parade, The, 72
PARABLES
  Good Shepherd, The, 68
  A Story Jesus Told, 73
RESURRECTION, THE
  First Easter, The, 75
SECOND COMING, THE
  I Will Come Again, 74
WALKING ON THE WATER
  Here Is the Boat, 61